Settling In

First Homes on the Prairies

Faye Reineberg Holt

FIFTH
HOUSE
PUBLISHERS

By the 1920s, many settlers had created beautiful yards and gardens at their farms.
Provincial Archives of Manitoba Agriculture—Farms–16

This homestead shack at Wainwright, Alberta, was so tiny that household essentials, such as the washtub, had to be stored on the exterior walls. City of Edmonton Archives 471–12

Here, in 1903, Mr. & Mrs. G.H. Shereman are shown arriving at their sod house in the Saskatchewan district of Tyvan.

The Tradition of Moving

Starting afresh in a new home has always been a part of prairie life. On today's prairies, moving vans and trucks piled with sofas, houseplants, TVs, and home computers speed along highways and trail dust on gravel roads. Before all this, before the days of modern conveniences, back when people had little and therefore travelled light, moving and settling in was every bit as common.

The nomadic First Nations people repeatedly took down existing homes and erected them somewhere else, season after season, one century after another. As the weather changed and the buffalo and fur-bearing animals moved on, the people packed their homes and belongings into buffalo-hide containers called parfleches and onto travois, teepee-pole frames pulled by dogs or horses. On the flat plains, along rivers, in the rolling hills, and in the wooded parkland, whole villages were taken apart, relocated, and rebuilt, again and again.

suit—missionaries settling in or near Native communities, and explorers, surveyors, and adventurers finding shelter in tents. Fur traders and Mounties built other kinds of homes, and finally, huge numbers of pioneer homes speckled the prairies.

Pioneer homes were as varied and innovative as housing is today. Sod walls provided only primitive shelter, and wood, stones, and bricks soon became the construction materials of choice. Some houses were elaborate, and even mansions made a

As newcomers from other cultures and places moved to western Canada, they had to adapt to the inhospitable prairie landscape. On the plains, for instance, there were scarcely any trees for lumber. The resourceful Native people had constructed teepees out of buffalo skins, and the first newcomers followed

The age of a soddie was indicated by the amount of plant growth on the roof. This shack, which boasted a veritable "crop" on top, was photographed in about 1910.

Saskatchewan Archives Board R–A 15292

surprisingly early appearance in the Canadian West.

The story of those first homes offers a glimpse of the exciting era when the West was settled. It also reveals construction methods fading into the past. More important, it is the story of dramatically diverse lifestyles and cultures and the inspiring process of turning very different dwellings into homes.

The earliest known home on the prairies is the teepee. The secrets and skills of building teepees from tanned buffalo hides and poles were passed among women from generation to generation. Men sometimes painted designs on the covers, but the homes belonged to the women. Cool in summer, stable in strong winds, dry in rainy weather, and warm in winter, teepees were valued possessions.

In general, the teepee was a cone-shaped lodging made of hide stretched over long poles. An interior lining, made of decorated hide, stretched from the floor halfway up the sides of the teepee, preventing drafts. At the same time, it created ideal air circulation: fresh air was drawn from under the bottom edge of the outer cover, pulled up through the gap between the exterior and interior layers, then swept up with any smoke escaping through the smoke flaps. These ingenious smoke flaps,

In 1910, these Doukhobor women at Veregin, Saskatchewan, mixed mud for plastering. They made the mud more adhesive by including straw or long grasses in the mixture.
Glenbow Archives NA 1037–4

This Native encampment shows numerous Red River carts and wagons to transport teepees. Note the wall tent in the centre right. Glenbow Archives NA 395–15

which opened near the tops of the poles, kept the home smoke-free, despite the fire situated in the middle of the teepee floor.

The floor was carpeted with cozy buffalo robes or the furs of other animals, and the families lounged against hand-woven willow backrests. Boxes were made of decorated rawhide. When the time came to move to a new hunting or trapping area, the people settled their teepees onto travois, packed their belongings into the parfleche boxes, secured the boxes to the travois, and left.

Fur Traders and First Settlers

Adapting to their surroundings wasn't quite as smooth for the newcomers to the prairies. At first, explorers and fur traders made temporary homes out of the tents they carried in their canoes or in their large, shallow York boats. The tents were available from eastern and European suppliers in numerous styles and sizes, but eventually the newcomers struggled to build permanent shelters.

During the fur-trade days, more than two hundred forts dotted the Northwest. Many were little more than log shacks housing only one or two traders. As the population of fur-bearing animals plummeted in areas, numerous forts were abandoned and fell into ruin.

Here, a lean-to has been added on to an older log cabin. Usually a small lean-to was built first; then a larger lumber home was added. South Saskatchewan Photo Museum

Some fur-trade forts were small communities, housing many people within the palisades. A large bachelor hall might sleep twenty or more clerks and traders. Traders' families, mostly Métis, usually lived in small wooden houses or in rows of rooms that were connected to the blacksmith's shop and quarters. According to Alexander Henry, at Fort Vermilion in 1810, that community numbered 130. House Number One slept seventeen people, including four men, four women, and nine children. Two dwellings each sheltered fifteen, one held fourteen, another housed eighteen, and another was home to ten. Two families lived together in a tent, and one family had its own tent. Those who ranked as company gentlemen were more fortunate, and a few had dwellings to themselves.[1]

Slowly, a sprinkling of farmers and settlers put up wooden homes around Fort Carlton, Fort Garry (which became Winnipeg), Fort Edmonton, and some of the other forts. Lord Selkirk, a Scottish nobleman and the first person to try a large-scale colony, planned a settlement at the Forks, which was near Fort Garry.

Having acquired 300,417 square kilometres (116,000 square miles) of land by 1811, Lord Selkirk hoped to attract poverty-stricken farmers and fishermen from Ireland and Scotland to his new community. He started by recruiting crofters who were being evicted in Scotland, and he sent an advance party of 106 men to build shelters for them.

The men reached York Factory, on the shore of Hudson Bay, late in September, but quarrels led to disaster. Their boats were carted back to England, so the first group camped for the winter and built new boats for their journey to the colony site.

The catastrophes continued. The next year, the second party of settlers and servants arrived late in the season and with inadequate tools and food. The third party, a hundred colonists, suffered from typhoid on the ocean voyage. Many died. Others were still sick when the ship's captain, perhaps in fear, abandoned them at Churchill, rather than deliver them to York Factory. Somehow, the settlers built a camp.

After barely surviving the winter, forty-one settlers set out on 6 April to walk the 241 kilometres (150 miles) to York Factory. With their own highland piper playing, twenty-one men and twenty women started out. On the way, one woman gave birth.

In late June 1814, after another 1200-kilometre (744-mile) trek by river to their new settlement, they began building their log cabins and settling in. Anxious to be rid of the settlers, North West Company fur traders used threats and enticements to lure all but thirteen families to Upper Canada. The homes of the loyal thirteen families were burned, but they and other newly arriving settlers somehow endured.

Between 1821 and 1825, the Red River Colony blossomed, especially with the addition of Swiss settlers and retired fur traders. Selkirk's original Scottish immigrants were finally outnumbered.

In 1823, fifteen hundred people resided in the settlement, and it continued to grow. Then 1826 brought deep snow. The following spring, the Red River rose and rose and rose. For more than twenty days during the massive flood, settlers abandoned their homes. They valiantly rescued others and moved livestock to higher ground. Many tried to save what little they could of their treasured tools and belongings. Almost all watched their homes float away. During the disaster, some settlers' effects were pilfered. No longer able to bear the hardships, 243 colonists left for the United States.[2]

Glad to be rid of them, the Hudson's Bay Company—which had granted Selkirk land for them in the first place—helped them to move out. Yet a few colonists remained, rebuilt homes in the same area, and again started farming with the barest of essentials. Despite the visionary colonization plan and phenomenal courage of the colonists, the first serious settlement attempt had suffered many setbacks. Still, some settlers were determined to remain and to survive.

Elsewhere on the prairies, a few surprisingly fine homes had been erected. At Fort Edmonton, Chief Factor John Rowand built the most elegant fur-trade dwelling west of Fort Garry. While the layout of the large fort was typical, Rowand's "Big House" was anything but typical.

Nicknamed "The Czar," the chief factor built his three-storey home on the hill above the fort. Jokingly called Rowand's Folly, it featured a ballroom. There, with their numerous servants, the chief factor and his Métis common-law wife, Louise, entertained governors, lords, dignitaries, renowned travellers, and missionaries. Unfortunately, like hundreds of other homes on the dry prairies, Rowand's Folly eventually went up in flames.

With the takeover of the North West Company by the Hudson's Bay Company in 1821, many fur-trade forts were abandoned. But other kinds of forts, which

After Chief Factor John Rowand's mansion burned down, the next chief factor, Richard Charles Hardisty, built another "Big House" at Fort Edmonton. In this 1884 photo, Hardisty's home, high on the hill, overlooks the barracks on the left.

Glenbow Archives NA 1315–16

resembled those of the fur trade, sprang up. On the southern plains, whisky forts housed illicit traders, and throughout the prairies, North West Mounted Police (NWMP) forts became home to the Mounties. As homes, the forts had similar weaknesses. The communal, barrack-style accommodations were drafty and cold in winter, and their roofs often leaked rain. Not surprisingly, this form of housing would virtually disappear. It was the individual, small homes built by the Selkirk settlers that foreshadowed the massive housing transformation on the horizon.

Cheap Land for Millions

During the mid- to late 1800s, settlers were lured west with various colonization schemes, among them the Dominion Lands Act. The Canadian government needed settlers in order to firm up its international boundaries. Railway builders needed customers for their existing and planned railways. Speculators and socially conscious visionaries, having formed colonization companies, had already started small colonies by buying land from the Hudson's Bay reserve. Eventually, the Crown acquired all but one-twentieth of the original Hudson's Bay lands, and populating the West began in earnest.

With aggressive homestead and immigration policies, prairie populations mushroomed. The greatest influx of immigrants occurred between 1910 and 1914. In 1911–1912, more than 136,000 immigrants arrived.
Provincial Archives of Alberta A 10,933

An Order-in-Council, 25 April 1871, established that a section of land would be 260 hectares or 2.6 square kilometres (640 acres or 1 square mile). A township would be thirty-six sections. As a result, throughout the West, government surveyors pounded in or built markers for sections, quarter sections, and townships.

By 1871, government-owned and surveyed lands were already available for a dollar per .4 hectare (1 acre) to colonization companies. Grazing leases were available for much less. The Dominion Lands Act, passed in 1872, set aside Native reserves and two sections per township for schools. Sub-sequently amended, it provided for land grants to Métis people, mining companies, and retirees from the military or the NWMP. Settlers born or residing in the North-West Territories before March 1870 could also claim lands. Railway companies became entitled to huge land grants for every 1.6 kilometres (1 mile) of railway built. Even more important, free land for homesteaders fired the imagina-tions of land-poor people around the world.

Any male or female British sub-ject, as well as anyone prepared to become a British subject, who was over eight-een and the sole head of a household, had only to pay a filing fee of ten dollars. On filing at a Dominion Lands Office, the home-steader would qualify for a free quarter sec-tion in western Canada. Homesteaders could also file a pre-emption, which allowed them to buy a neighbouring quarter section once they had proven their own homestead. Immigrants had to file for themselves in Canada, although a father, brother, son, or sister could file for a family member by proxy. The homesteader had to cultivate the land and live on it six months a year for three years.

From early spring to late fall, surveyors with the Boundary Commission (1872–1874) lived in wagons and tents. Settlers also used tents and wagons as temporary homes. Provincial Archives of Manitoba N11931

Land-poor immigrants and those escaping religious persecution flooded Canadian ports of entry. Eastern Canadians and Americans were equally excited about possibilities. Nervous that all the land in a certain area might become claimed, many filed on land sight unseen. Others searched for a desirable quarter and hoped to reach a land office before someone else filed on it.

At the same time, railways received land for proposed rail lines. The giant amongst them, the Canadian Pacific Railway (CPR), wanted to tackle a transcontinental line, and as an incentive, it received huge chunks of land. For the

This miniature 1906 dwelling must have been very inexpensive. Most turn-of-the-century homesteaders paid $150 to $300 for housing materials and transportation of the materials to homesteads.
Saskatchewan Archives Board R–A 2336

right price, desirable locations along the CPR line were sold to settlers. Soon the concerted advertising and recruiting efforts of the Canadian government, the CPR, and colonization companies made western Canada the talk of Britain, Europe, and the northwestern American states. Although not everybody trusted the motives of the advertisers, thousands of people flocked to the Canadian prairies.

Once in Canada, individuals and their families pushed west by steamship across the Great Lakes, by rail as far as possible, and then by wagon. When the railroad extended into Manitoba and no farther, that province experienced the first significant influx of people.

One of the many eastern Canadian families to make the journey was the family of John Mooney and Elizabeth Scott Mooney, who farmed stony land in Grey County, Ontario. In 1879, Will, the eldest of their six children, headed west to scout for land. He filed on quarter sections for himself, his father, and his brother. The family soon followed, by ship, rail, and wagon.

Their daughter Nellie—who would later become famous as

Nellie McClung—was six when they made the trip. On reaching St. Boniface, the reunited family camped temporarily in a tent at the junction of the Red and Assiniboine Rivers. Then Elizabeth and her younger children moved into a local house while her husband and older sons left to build a cabin on their land. Finally, the men returned for them. With a Red River cart, a cow, and two wagonloads of possessions pulled by two oxen, the family set off for their cabin in the woods.

They travelled with other settlers during the fourteen-day trip. Their wagons rolled through mud and across the Assiniboine and then the Souris River. After a short dis-

tance, Nellie viewed her new home.

The log house had a thatched roof, made from prairie hay and was not chinked, but it had a floor of rough lumber ... and one window. One window might be thought insufficient for a house that must lodge eight people, but light and air came in unbidden through many openings; indeed how to keep out the cold became our great problem.

That first winter was long and cruel. Isolation, heavy snows, and illness created even more hardship. Nellie's eldest sister caught a cold. Their mother hung quilts behind her bed to keep away drafts, but the illness intensified. "My girl is dying for want of a doctor in this cursed place—that never should have been taken from the Indians," she cried.

Then a Methodist minister arrived, bedecked in fur coat and snowshoes and with one cheek frozen, but also bearing medicine, which led to Nellie's sister's recovery.[3]

The free land in Canada attracted people from around the world. Some ethnic or religious

Notched logs fit together tightly at the corners of this building, constructed near Drumheller, Alberta, in the early 1900s. Large logs were used for both stable and house. Elsewhere, some people travelled eighty kilometres (fifty miles) even for firewood. Glenbow Archives NA 2612–24

groups, such as Russian German and Ukrainian families, had already tried living in South America, but there they had to contend with disease and hostility from the Native South Americans. Dr. Joseph Oleskow, a Ukrainian professor, investigated Canada. With support from the Canadian government, the CPR, and his colleagues, he encouraged Ukrainian families to move to the Canadian North-West Territories.

After a ten-day ocean crossing, then a train trek from Halifax or Montreal, many Ukrainians settled near Winnipeg and in the Fort Saskatchewan and Edmonton areas of Alberta.

In 1897, John Hryhorczuk moved his family of four from the village of Balynets to near Dauphin, Manitoba. He modelled their temporary shelter on those used in the highlands of Ukraine. First he cut the tops off two five-metre (sixteen-foot) trees but left a "crutch" on each. Then he set a ridgepole across them and leaned other poles against the ridgepole. He covered this roof with hay and bark, set a store-bought window in the gable, and made a door from a blanket.

The family spent the summer there while John went away to work. It was too late for a garden but Mrs. Hryhorczuk had chickens and food staples. They picked berries, and got milk from a neighbour.

The shelter's roof leaked, and rain seeped in, but there was little to damage. Unfortunately, the family's good clothes and linens had been lost during the ocean voyage.

That summer, mother and son cleared land for a new home and garden. Finally, John returned with a cow and two steers. Before winter, with the help of neighbours, he built a new home, which was made of lumber.[4]

A home doesn't have to be fancy! These folks found adequate summer shelter in a pole-and-branch creation. National Archives of Canada PAC 178587, CNR Collection

Mansions and Missions

Dating back to the very early days of white settlement, the West also boasted various stone homes, as well as mansions. John Turriff, born in Quebec, where stone houses were common, ordered up a huge stone home in 1883. The previous year, in the Moose Mountain area of what would become southern Saskatchewan, he had built a general store with his living quarters at the back. The community of Carlyle grew around him as homesteaders arrived. Hailing from Ontario and Manitoba, most built log homes.

This rare house was built by an Estonian family in 1910 near Foremost, Alberta. By 1901, only seventeen Alberta homes had been constructed of stone. More than ten thousand were made of wood. Glenbow Archives NA 2616–36

By 1884, the twenty-eight-year-old Turriff was married and elected to the territorial legislature. He moved his family into the stone mansion. Built by stonemason Ben Hollonquist, the impressive house had three storeys, a back kitchen for storage, a meat house, and a milk house—all of stone. The basement even had a well.

Some mansions, most of them at Fort Garry (Winnipeg), predated Turriff's stone home. Silver Heights was the home of Donald Smith, chief commissioner of the Hudson's Bay Company, and later a railway tycoon, member of the Manitoba legislature, and member of Parliament.

Considered the most lavish manor in the West, Silver Heights overlooked the Assiniboine River. There, Smith's guests enjoyed lawns, flowers, trellised arbours, gabled stables, and parties, parties, parties.[5] As violins played the Blue Danube in the second-floor ballroom, romantic figures waltzed the night away.

Even this could not please Lady Dufferin, whose husband, England's Lord Dufferin, was Governor General of Canada from 1872 to 1878. When they visited Manitoba in 1877 and stayed at Silver Heights, Lady Dufferin wrote:

Our house is a cottage . . . The A.D.C.s [aides-de-camp] are in a smaller cottage close by, and the men-servants sleep in tents. A fine reception room, and two anti-rooms [ante-rooms], carpeted, papered, and furnished, have been added to the house for us, which we regret as the place is really too far away to entertain in; nor have we the china, or the knives and forks, wherewith to give a ball or dinner![6]

In 1924, this Winnipeg, Manitoba, mansion belonging to Augustus Nanton featured an elegantly decorated music room. Provincial Archives of Manitoba N15396
Winnipeg-Homes-Nanton Augustus Meredith 28

Lady Dufferin remained unimpressed even at Government House, the splendid home of Lieutenant-Governor Morris. Another inconvenience was the eight-kilometre (five-mile) trip to Winnipeg over a "sort of track on the prairie." The mud, she said, was knee-deep. Even while just climbing into the carriage, "we were very much damaged; feathers out of curl, dresses dirtied."

While her expectations were high for the refined likes of herself, Lady Dufferin's expectations were markedly lower for the housing of new immigrants in "the colonies."

Two Galician men from Ukraine built this homestead house in Saskatchewan during the summer of 1908. Like most Ukrainian homes, it was plastered inside and out. Typically, the two- or three-room homes were single-storey and faced south. Saskatchewan Archives Board R–A 9690

During a visit to a Russian German Mennonite village, where 120 families had settled in 1874, she wrote:

Necessity [in Russia] has taught them to make peculiar fuel-cakes of manure mixed with straw—which is kept a whole year to dry . . . with this they get through the long Canadian winter without wood or coal . . . The houses are cottages, very plainly built, roofed with very thick hay thatch, the walls wooden, but covered with plaster. Next to, and opening into the living-house is a large building in which the cattle spend the winter. Everything looks very neat; home-made wooden furniture, flowers in the windows, nice gardens . . .[7]

Hundreds of other Eastern European settlers built similar first homes. Most homes were log, chinked and plastered with mud, whitewashed, and topped with beautiful and intricately thatched roofs. The women usually created the mud, chinked, plastered, and whitewashed, while the men worked the land or took other jobs to pay for farm buildings, equipment, and livestock.

Emily Ferguson Murphy began her sojourn in western Canada in the early 1900s. She and her husband, Arthur, were born in eastern Canada. He had been an internationally renowned Anglican evangelist, and the family spent two years in England and Europe. In about 1906, they moved near Swan River, Manitoba. After visiting the Doukhobor village of Vosnesenia [Voznesenie], Saskatchewan, she wrote of the wide street separating houses and of the drainage ditches on each side of the village. The one-storey houses were "foreign in every line," but the strangeness was not a negative trait. "They are . . . frescoed with vivid dadoes [grooves or slots cut into the boards]. Sometimes the roofs project into verandas, which are ornamented with carving." Thick layers of hemp created blinds, which were hung on the outside of windows. Inside, the homes were decorated with brown and yellow dadoes, coloured pictures, and calendars, and there were flowers in the deep windowsills.[8]

To her, the houses of Eastern Europeans suited the landscape, unlike the tool-box-style homes built for and by other newcomers.

The architecture here is early Western style and possesses the high art of simplicity. The people here are in such haste to get to work they have no time for building houses, and so are content with shells—"shacks" they call them. They are such houses as Thoreau described as a tool-box with a few auger holes bored in it to admit light, and a hook to fasten down the lid at night.[9]

Mostly Eastern Europeans and Russians plastered their homes. Here, Doukhobor women work on a log house. A good plaster job usually required three layers, with the last worked to a smooth finish. Saskatchewan Archives Board S–A 129

At the time, homes for Anglican ministers in the West looked like tool boxes and followed rigid building specifications. Financed by the church, each house came in a kit, was assembled on site, and measured 3.6 metres by 5.4 metres (12 feet by 18 feet). Its roof sloped from the 3.6-metre-high (12-foot) front wall to the 3-metre-high (10-foot) back. The kit included numbered boards and two glass windows. The floor was to be covered with tarpaper, and the walls and roof were double-papered.

Nicknamed Lambeth Palaces, after the London residence of the Archbishop of Canterbury, each cost $150. According to plan, once the parish could afford a larger home, the new parsonage should be built in front of the old, with the old one becoming a lean-to or kitchen.[10]

Between the 1880s and the 1920s, not only ministers but thousands of others found themselves living in similar tool boxes and in worse conditions. The trickle of settlers had become a flood, thanks to the aggressive advertising campaigns of the Canadian government, the CPR, and the colonization companies. With such inadequate services, transportation, supplies, and building materials on the prairies, the settlers built whatever kinds of houses they could cobble together.

This dwelling, photographed about 1918, was a popular, low-cost design used for homesteads and missions throughout the prairies. Provincial Archives of Alberta Harry Pollard P 592

Tarpaper helped to keep moisture and wind out of lumber and log homes. Building paper was also used inside homes. Often it was then covered with another layer of newspaper or wallpaper.

Saskatchewan Archives Board R–A 7226–1

Making a Profit

By 1882, for two dollars per .4 hectare (1 acre), payable within five years, private colonization companies could buy land from the government within thirty-nine kilometres (twenty-four miles) of the main CPR line or within nineteen kilometres (twelve miles) of a branch railway line. The colonization companies had two options. In one option, they could pay up-front for the land. In the other plan, they could take five years to pay but were required to place more settlers on the land.

The number of colonization companies doubled and doubled again. Twenty-six colonization companies had bought 1.2 million hectares (almost 3 million acres) by 1883.[11] Among them were the York Farmers' Colonization Company near Yorkton, Saskatchewan; Dominion Lands Colonization Company; the Primitive Methodist

Colonization Company; Touchwood and Qu'Appelle Colonization Company; and Montreal and Western Lands Company.

Even though the companies usually sold land for double what they paid, the land prices still appealed to established farmers. Aggressive companies recruiting American settlers sometimes offered lavish excursions to their properties for potential buyers. By 1912, the Wm. Pearson Company had conducted excursions of more than one hundred people to Last Mountain Valley, Saskatchewan. On Sundays, it entertained excursionists at the nearby lake with parties on the company's steamship or beach activities and fishing at its summer resort.[12]

Companies seemed to spring up overnight, but many failed almost as quickly. Unpopular with Canadians, colonization company grants were not available

after 1886 and existing contracts were terminated. The Saskatchewan Land and Colonization Company, for example, had held about 200,000 hectares (about 500,000 acres) near Yorkton, Saskatchewan, and Red Deer, Alberta. It had paid just over $150,000 but had established only 245 settlers. As a final settlement, the Canadian government gave the company final title to about 48,000 hectares (about 120,000 acres) and scrip entitlements to $32,000 worth of additional land. The rest reverted to the government.[13]

Without the federal grants, in the years that followed, some colonization companies purchased land from the railway companies. One such company was the Canadian American Land Company, formed in 1901 by some investors from North Dakota. It resold farmland in present-day Alberta and Saskatchewan. By 1906, some

On 4 June 1912, these potential settlers viewed land in Last Mountain Valley, Saskatchewan. Travelling single file in up to thirty-five rigs, they covered about sixty-five to eighty kilometres (forty to fifty miles) each day with the Wm. Pearson Company. *Provincial Archives of Manitoba Settlement N4944*

of those investors formed another company, the Calgary Colonization Company. Its Rosebud Tract encompassed 121,500 hectares (300,000 acres) in central Alberta. There, the company built four large farms to showcase the area's farming potential. Near Beiseker, one of its farms provided new settlers and their livestock with temporary shelter. Women and children slept in the house, while men slept in a huge tent. By 1918, Hutterites had bought one of the original Calgary Colonization Company farms for their new colony on the Rosebud River.

At Cannington Manor, Saskatchewan, these bachelors spruced up their humble log abode with pictures on the walls. South Saskatchewan Photo Museum

Over the next decade, Americans and Germanic people settled in the Beiseker area. Some travelled endlessly to get there, only to discover friends from back home. The George Uffelman family left Russia in 1906 and spent seven years in Buenos Aires, Argentina. In 1913, the family started for Canada, first journeying by ship to England, then recrossing the Atlantic to New York. From New York, they travelled by train to Calgary. Arriving in Calgary after forty-four days of travel, they were surprised to meet a friend from Russia. Eventually, they settled with other Russian Germans near Beiseker.[14]

Many prairie homesteaders sent money overseas to their relatives so that the relatives could afford to join them in Canada. The relatives would then live with the homesteaders until they could buy their own land nearby and build a house. Because of this, and because of colonization schemes, many communities developed strong bonds of culture, language, values, religion, and politics.

Hungarian families settled at Esterhazy, Saskatchewan. At nearby Sumner Colony, a dozen Irish, English, and Scottish families settled. According to Christina Willey, the settlers built a log post office and community hall, and Mrs. Sumner became second

For two weeks in 1903, the Barr colonists camped at Saskatoon. Not only were the tents temporary homes, one was a fully equipped hospital tent.
Saskatchewan Archives Board R–B 1361

English colonists and acquired blankets, tents, and other military supplies left over from the Boer War.

In 1903, the optimistic group began the trek from Saskatoon to their land about 278 kilometres (173 hundred miles) away on the Saskatchewan-Alberta border at today's Lloydminster. Unfortunately, only a few had experience with horses, and none had ever worked with oxen. When the colonists reached their land, some built homes of log and some of lumber. Others had neither the materials nor the know-how to build adequate homes.

mother to all the bachelors, treating them to special meals. Despite the privations of pioneer life and the loss of her china on the voyage, Willey found everything orderly and well-kept in the colony—sometimes too well-kept. Her sister-in-law washed the log walls, scrubbed her painted floor down to the white boards, and once made Willey sit with her feet on newspaper to keep the floor clean!

Other prairie colonists arrived very ill-prepared and faced a devastating change in lifestyle. Wanting to establish an all-British colony, Rev. Isaac Barr recruited two thousand

A few tried building sod houses, but their soddies were poorly constructed. Eventually, the Mounties and a doctor helped many Barr colonists move into two huge marquee tents. In one tent, blankets were used to separate thirty families into small cubicles. The other tent was packed with single men.

Many of the single men left, but the men and families who stayed eventually prospered after Barr was replaced as leader by his rival, Rev. George Lloyd (after whom Lloydminster was named).[15]

Tents and Tent Towns

With the influx of settlers, tent towns sprang up at major stops on the railway. Many homesteaders arrived too late in the season to build wooden or sod homes before winter, so they congregated in canvas tents in Winnipeg, Regina, Saskatoon, Edmonton, and Calgary. During cold snaps, some even discovered that water heating on the stove could freeze before it boiled. But at least these new-comers lived close to stores and schools.

For those who had filed for homestead rights sight unseen, locating their land the next spring was sometimes tricky. They could hire local finders to read and locate survey markers. If the homesteaders arrived at their land early enough in the season, they could plough, sow, build homes, and harvest before the first snowflake fell. If they arrived late in the season—unorganized and

In about 1910, the tent town near Jasper, Alberta, included a tent hotel, other eating establishments, and a barbershop. Glenbow Archives NA 1679–12

also naïve about winter's brutality—they were blindsided when the weather turned cold. Hospitable neighbours often took pity and offered them shelter, either in their crowded houses or in abandoned shacks or granaries. Some settlers tried spending the winter in tents on their own land.

The Jim MacGregor family arrived in Edmonton from Scotland during October 1906.

The E.A. Smith family lived in this tent around 1909. During the summer, cookstoves were often placed outside tents. Provincial Archives of Alberta A 2537

Mrs. MacGregor and their one-year-old boy, John, joined dozens of women and children of all nationalities camped on Ross Flats while her husband prospected for a homestead.

At the MacGregor site, boxes of household items, clothes, and fine china awaited delivery to the family's new home. Finally, Jim MacGregor returned with Tom Pirie, whose family was also camped at the tent town. The two families would soon be neighbours on their homesteads.

Without horses or oxen, the MacGregors hired a ride to their new home, seventy-four kilometres (forty-six miles) northwest of Edmonton. By the evening of 21 October, the tent had been pitched on their land, and Jim MacGregor had made a spruce-bough bed for his family. The quarter section was heavily wooded with tall spruce, which would provide logs for a good home, and Jim looked forward to building his farm. Mrs. MacGregor, on the other hand, already regretted their decision to homestead.

The next day, as she unpacked trunks, she was even more downcast. Saltwater from the voyage had ruined clothing. Most of her everyday dishes were broken. So were all but a dozen pieces of her Dresden and Royal Doulton china. She could do nothing but throw the shards behind the tent.

In the days that followed, husband and wife felled trees and dug a cellar for a large house. Then the snow began. The immigration literature had hinted at unpredictable winters, and a neighbour was alarmed at the weather, so the MacGregors quickly positioned their tent over the new cellar.

The winter of 1906–1907 proved to be one of the worst on record. One night, the stovepipe became blocked, filling the tent with smoke and driving the family out into the snow. Another problem was Mrs. MacGregor's inexperience as a bread baker. With one failure after another, the flour and other supplies dwindled.

In 1910, Tom Qually lived in a gable-roofed dugout in Groton, Alberta. When banked with deep snow, animals walked over such dwellings. Glenbow Archives NA 2616–17

By mid-January 1907, the MacGregors were in serious danger but too proud to ask neighbours for help. Mr. MacGregor cut and split a huge pile of wood and then set out on foot for Edmonton. After he found a job there, he would send a team to fetch his wife and son.

Snow piled high around the tent, but inside, the anxious mother and her child were warm. As Mrs. MacGregor marked off each day, rationing her matches, one week stretched into two, coyotes howled at night, and animals left tracks outside the tent.

One evening, her fear rose to terror. A wild animal had followed the incline of the snowbank to the top of the tent. In the lamplight, she could see the shape settle near the warm stovepipe. The animal's claws scratched at the canvas. She held her baby tightly, her eyes glued to the shape until it disappeared the next morning.

She cried most of that next day. To her horror, the shape returned that evening, again curling up in the same warm spot. For hours, she endured paralysing fear.

Finally, she picked up the .303 gun, put it against her shoulder, and fired. The blast seemed deafening. The gun's recoil bruised her shoulder and knocked her across the bed. The shape was gone, but Mrs. MacGregor was still consumed with fear.

The next day, she bundled herself and her baby in their warmest clothes and set out for the neighbour's place. The Piries lived a scant kilometre (about half a mile) away, but Mrs. MacGregor—born and raised in London—was not familiar with the outdoors. Carrying her baby, she followed the trail signs her husband had blazed in standing timber. Then, detouring around deadfall, she became lost.

She hugged John closely as she stumbled through deep drifts and over logs. Tripping, she dropped him in the snow. She picked him up and continued her search for help. Finally, after two hours, she found the Piries' shack and safety.

The next day, they arranged for another neighbour, with a wagon, to take her to Edmonton, where she located her husband without even having his address. He had, in fact, sent a teamster for them, but the teamster had arrived after Mrs. MacGregor and baby John had left. Like thousands of others, however, the MacGregors returned to their land the next spring and made it their home.[16]

Nothing but Dirt

On the southern prairies, the Great Plains, many newcomers confronted seemingly impossible situations. Unlike their neighbours on the central and northern prairies, these pioneers lacked the luxury of trees for building materials and firewood. Few had envisioned the wide-open, flat, barren, unpopulated landscape. How could they build a home, with only the ground beneath their feet?

Some settlers had left a similar landscape in the American northwest, where they or their parents had lived in sod homes. Many Doukhobors, Ukrainians, and Mennonites had also lived in earthen homes or had acquired this precious knowledge from parents or grandparents. But other pioneers simply learned the art and science of soddie construction at the school of hard knocks.

During construction of this sod home, guide poles indicated the intended height of the walls.
Glenbow Archives NA 474–2

In April 1901, J.A. Rankel and his family moved from Gretna, Manitoba, to homestead near Weyburn, Saskatchewan. They were greeted only by open space and some friendly neighbours. Good Samaritans were already a tradition on the prairies, and with winter approaching, a neighbour let the Rankels sleep in his stone home. The Rankels and their kind neighbour quickly erected a temporary shelter, but it would never be warm enough for winter.

Butter was often churned and laundry washed outside, rather than in the small, dark early homes. In about 1903, Mrs. H. Biggs sat churning butter at the Springfield Ranch near Beynon, Alberta. Glenbow Archives NC 43–12

Settlers soon became accustomed to scrounging around for wood, and one of the Rankels' neighbours had stumbled across a log cabin furnished solely with a bunk. Assuming the cabin was abandoned, he dismantled the logs and loaded them on his wagon. As he headed towards home with the wagonload of logs, he met and innocently chatted with a cowboy who had been riding the range. Days later, facing a Mountie on his doorstep, the settler learned the deserted cabin had belonged to the cowboy. Charged with theft and ordered to appear in court, the neighbour ran for the border, rather than serve whatever sentence the judge deemed harsh enough for stealing someone's home.

Lumber being in obviously short supply, the Rankels started an earthen home. For sod, they wisely selected a partially dried-up slough with good growth. The most suitable sod was just porous enough for native grasses to send down tightly entangled roots, which held the soil in place.

As his father ploughed furrows, the eldest Rankel boy followed with a stoneboat. With a saw, he cut sod and hauled it to the site of their new home. There, his father built a 4.2-by-6-metre (14-by-20-foot) enclosure with walls 2.7 metres

(9 feet) high. What precious wood they had scrounged they used for the roof, which they piled with hay.

Inside, the two boys plastered the walls with mud, and their mother applied the finishing coat. She eventually whitewashed the walls, which were .6 to 1.2 metres (2 to 4 feet) thick. The well-insulated sod home, snug and warm throughout the winter, proved warmer than the lumber home the Rankels were later able to build.[17]

Heavy rainfall could cause serious problems in sod homes. In the worst-case scenarios, the weight of rain-drenched sod collapsed roofs on settlers and their belongings. In almost all soddies, for days after a rain, the roof dripped. To solve the problem, the Rankels finally shingled their roof, but other pioneers perfected a layering technique. They set poles or lumber across the top of the sod walls, placed tarpaper over the wood, and then layered sod

on top, with the grass facing the interior. Next they might add a layer of grass or hay. On the outermost layer of sod, the grass grew skyward.

Construction methods for soddies varied widely. Some settlers simply made dugouts with roofs. Others carved into the sides of hills, which became natural roofs. Still others created above-ground sod homes with ground-level cellars.

One cellar-type home of mixed materials was built in 1884 near Edenwold, Saskatchewan. The grandfather of R. Milesby dug a hole about a metre (three feet) deep. Next, he built a gable-style roof by leaning other poles against a ridgepole. Then, he piled a foot of hay over the structure and finished the roof with squares of sod.

But not all dirt was equal when it came to constructing a sturdy sod home. Soil with too much sand or not enough

This sod and lumber home belonged to Menno Moyer, who homesteaded near Redvers, Saskatchewan, about 1908. Saskatchewan Archives Board R–A 7555

root growth didn't stand up to wind and rain. Clara Hoffer and her husband settled near Byrne, Saskatchewan, where they built their new home. A strong wind buffeted the walls, the sod slid, and all their work was for naught.

An above-ground, sod-roof structure capped a sunken floor near Coronation, Alberta, about 1907. Glenbow Archives NA 474–3

Sturdily constructed homes made from tough turf could stand for years. Generally, dugouts and soddies were intended as shelter for a mere year or two. By then, settlers expected to build better houses. But if crops failed or cash was short, a year might stretch to three or four before the family built another home.

Some homes were entirely sod; others included mixed construction materials, and in some cases, settlers used sod only as insulation along drafty wooden walls. Most above-ground structures were sod and either log or lumber,

but many were a mix of all three. The majority of these strange homes were built after 1875 but before improved transportation brought in other construction materials. By 1914, the soddie era had ended.

In contrast, early wealthy Calgary settlers built mansions out of a different construction material found in the ground: sandstone, hauled from nearby quarries. Eventually jobs at the quarries or in sandstone construction meant work for half of Calgary's tradespeople. Most of the sandstone buildings were places of business, but a few well-off Calgarians built sandstone mansions. The home built for William Pearce in 1899 had three fireplaces. The bathroom had running water, and there was a pool room in the basement. Built in 1901, Pat Burns's home was even more elegant.

FAMOUS CLYDESDALE BREEDING ESTABLISHMENT

"DOUNE LODGE," ARCOLA, SASK.

(For ownership see under pad.)

At Doune Lodge, near Arcola, Saskatchewan, this twelve-room house was built of rock in 1897. The farm, which was well-known for breeding Clydesdale horses, also featured rock construction on the bottom section of the barn walls.

South Saskatchewan Photo Museum

After the 1886 fire that devastated much of Calgary, homes built of quarried sandstone became popular with the wealthy living there. Senator James Lougheed's residence, Beaulieu, was built in 1892.

Glenbow Archives NA 789–157

The Trials of Everyday Life

Although some early homes were large, well-insulated, and comfortable, most were not. For instance, a soddie interior could be very dark, and families in windowless soddies depended entirely on lamps and candles for light. Some earthen homes did have framed windows. Others had mere slits for windows, covered with greased paper. They allowed in very little sunshine but lots of cold air.

Pioneer women found ingenious ways to brighten the atmosphere and to keep the dirt and insects from coming into the room. Some covered the walls and ceiling with layers of newspaper or real wallpaper. Many, like Margaret Stewart, hung whatever fabric they had—including curtains or sheets—around the walls and under the ceiling. Most hung pictures and calendars on the walls. Despite living in a soddie, some women still served meals on white tablecloths. Mrs. E.A. Bullis, who settled by the North Saskatchewan River about 225 kilometres (140 miles) from Edmonton, had to sit

Well-built soddies were pretty sturdy, but Mrs. C. Bull's home near McLaughlin, Alberta, was slammed by a tornado. Glenbow Archives NA 1662–5

on a nail keg for meals, but she used her good china and sterling silver utensils.

Immigration literature advised against bringing large items of furniture, such as pianos. Most settlers were poor and had neither the belongings nor the money for such extravagances. Once at the town nearest their new homesteads, settlers bought necessities including pails, basins, stoves, and stovepipes. Before setting out, they packed the essentials high on their wagons.

A fortunate few, especially those from the United States, did bring treasured pieces of furniture—including pianos. Some Eastern Europeans brought ornately carved and painted chests. Most bought Canadian-made chairs, tables, and cupboards. Some constructed them soon after they arrived, and others simply made do. They used packing crates as small cupboards, tables, and chairs. But even these could be painted to make them cheerful additions to homes.

Generally, both the sod homes and log cabins of early settlers were small and had few walls. Blankets and sheets became room dividers for children and parents, boys and

Homesteaders didn't necessarily abandon a life of gentility, even if their home was a tent. For lunch in this tent in 1900, at the W. Wright homestead near Calgary, the hostess used a white tablecloth. The well-dressed guests and hosts all sport stiff white collars, too. Glenbow Archives NA 1126–6

girls. If the family didn't have bedsteads and mattresses, simple bench-style beds were easy enough to build from a little lumber. Two pieces of heavyweight material sewn into a huge rectangle and filled with straw became a mattress. Flour sacks, worn-out clothes, and other fabric scraps became quilts. Flour sacks were filled with chicken feathers for pillows, and bits of material were woven into rugs.

Unfortunately, not all problems were easily solved in early prairie homes. Soddies suffered from worms, bugs, and snakes

In 1916, Joe Wacha and his wife plastered their log home about 6.5 kilometres (4 miles) north of Vita, Manitoba. They appear to have used mud for plaster and chinking. Logs not allowed to dry for about a year would shrink and the job had to be redone. Provincial Archives of Manitoba W.J. Sisler Collection 118 N9631

Justina Deering, also Russian German settlers. The elder Deerings had begun homesteading in a soddie. Then, working side by side, the two built a three-bedroom log-and-thatch home, where Nathaniel and Justina raised eleven children. This new home, with a foundation of rock and dirt, was plastered and then washed with kalsomine, which resembled white paint, inside and out. The old soddie was divided into a coal shed and chicken house, and farm life was good but demanding.

In addition to the house kitchen, the Deerings had an attached summer kitchen with a clay oven built from homemade bricks. Both kitchens had mud floors, as hard as concrete and easy to sweep. Exposed to weather and not painted on the outside, the summer kitchen's exterior had to be remudded each year. Even Liz's six-year-old son helped by riding the horse in circles to mix the dirt, water, and straw in one area.

The Deerings contended with flies and mice, and even reptiles crept into the house. One salamander, which became a pet, lived in a dish of water. Snakes found their way through the rock foundation and the thatched

dropping from ceilings or crawling out of walls. Log cabins, especially those with thatched roofs, had similar inconveniences.

Liz Boschéé Deering's family experienced a long history of settlement and hardship. Her German ancestors had moved to Russia, and her grandparents later moved to South Dakota. When her father was only four, the family moved to Walsh and later to Thelma, both near the Cypress Hills in Alberta. Liz grew up and married there, and the young couple lived with her in-laws, Nathanial and

roof. Once, Liz found five garter snakes in the house. Her worst snake memory was the day she found a .75-metre (2.5-foot) specimen winding its way down from the top of her cupboard. Liz killed the snake and later learned that, had it remained in the house much longer, it would have given birth to twenty-two babies!

Despite all the wildlife, Liz found joy in home decorating. She bought rolls of easy-to-wash oilcloth, commonly used for table-cloths, and pasted it to the bottom half of the walls, using glue made of flour and water. The decorating job—green and white oil-cloth on the lower half of the walls, sparkling white paint on the top half—lasted for years.[18]

Wooden homes weren't ideal, either, but log and lumber shacks of every imaginable sort were the most common early housing on the prairies, and many were infested with bedbugs. The bugs arrived in settlers' bedding or effects, or perhaps the lumber itself, and stayed in the home forever, becoming the plague of every successive family to live there. A family would use a house and then abandon it, either because they had given up or had built or found a better home. Other people soon moved in, and sometimes they shared the house with still other families in need.

The bedbugs could remain on the rafters of a house for years, sometimes long after the house was empty. When newcomers settled in, the bugs made their way to the beds. In the area around Red Deer, Alberta, as in many areas during the settlement boom, one mother awoke to find her tiny infant's face covered with bedbug bites.

To prevent the bugs from reaching the beds, another prairie mother painted coal oil along the iron rails and fittings of the beds. At night, she held the lamp directly under the

Eager to beautify their plain slab home in Bingley, Alberta, the Ogden family built a cold frame and planted vines. Vertical log construction shown in this 1911 photo was not common on the prairies.

Glenbow Archives NA 470–2

rafters and moved along slowly, catching the falling bedbugs in the lamp globe. Bedbugs were most voracious in the summer, and to escape the pests, this family slept in the granary. As soon as possible, the family moved to a new home. Without today's insecticides, the pests were almost impossible to eliminate unless the house was burned down.

Lice also kept the pioneers company, and they were passed along by hospitality. Few respectable pioneers would dream of refusing shelter to newcomers. Sometimes the only space available was in the barn or sheds, but whenever possible, immigrants were offered a bed or space in the house. Many had travelled in crowded ships and found shelter in Canadian immigration halls before reaching their homesteads. Lice on one person's clothes or bedding soon infested everyone, necessitating an attack with a kerosene rub or a kerosene-lard rub. Washable clothes and bedding were scrubbed with lots of boiling-hot water and soap, but mattresses had to be burned.

And the flies! They absolutely tormented the pioneers, few of whom had screen doors. Since fly swatters were a slow solution, many settlers used flypaper strips or black, poisonous pads that, when covered with water and left in saucers, looked like syrup. The poison was simply too dangerous for young children, though, so families flapped at the flies with leafy branches and tea towels, shooing the pests out the door.

Mice and moths also moved in with homesteaders, the mice nibbling on foodstuffs and the moths nibbling on clothes. Housekeepers had to remain ever vigilant against unwanted guests.

A recluse used whatever scraps and natural materials he could scavenge to build his home near Halbrite, Saskatchewan, in 1928.
South Saskatchewan Photo Museum

Fewer Hardships

Homesteading wasn't such tough sledding for everybody. A few pioneers had enough money to build lumber homes soon after their arrival. Some American immigrants simply moved their old houses to Canada.

In fact, many established American farmers were tempted north by the prospect of cheap—or free—land. Colonization companies targeted farmers in Minnesota, Wisconsin, Nebraska, and North and South Dakota. Those farmers had money, and they could sell their

In 1935, this homestead house was moved on the streets of Edmonton, Alberta. Families often economized by moving their old house, rather than building or buying a new one.
City of Edmonton Archives 160–961

established farms for substantial profits. Then they could file for one homestead quarter in Canada and acquire others from the CPR or colonization companies.

The Canadian government paid freight for settlers' effects, so some clever Americans filled more than one boxcar with belongings. Some, such as Mary Grutman's family, even packed their houses. The original Grutman farm, southwest of Minneapolis, was taken apart by workers in 1907. They numbered boards and even counted and crated the bricks for the chimney. They also packed doors, windows, and frames.[19]

Since the move cost nothing, a few Americans packed up their barns and blacksmith shops. They loaded their farms and animals on boxcars and shipped them across the border. Once the effects were unloaded at the station nearest to the new farms, the immigrants hauled everything to the homestead.

Well aware of the challenges of winter, the Americans timed their move carefully and made the trip in spring. They were prepared to live in tents in the summer, ploughing, planting, harvesting, and reconstructing their farms. If their new homes weren't ready in the fall, they simply returned to the States and spent the winter with friends or relatives. For them, homesteading in Canada required less money, physical effort, and hardship because they didn't have to start from scratch.

Mail-order Homes

Prefabricated homes were a boon to many homesteaders. Shipped in boxes and bundles, the houses were built on farms and homesteads throughout the West. Included in the package were doors, windows, frames, mouldings, casements, lath, finishing lumber, tarpaper, and shingles. In addition, settlers could order plumbing and heating packages for a few hundred dollars more.

By 1908, Sears Roebuck in the United States was selling mail-order homes. The CPR soon joined in, and by 1912, the T. Eaton Company had hopped on board. Eaton's homes were available only in the three Prairie provinces, and the company continued the service until 1932.

For one dollar, a customer could order blueprints, which were worth between twenty-five and seventy-five dollars in 1918. Once

This prefab farmhouse, used by a southern Alberta family in 1913, was CPR House Plan Number 4. Once ordered from the railway company, the materials were shipped to the railway station nearest the homesteader. Glenbow Archives NA–2829–12

the customer ordered the package, Eaton's refunded the dollar. Customers could also opt to send their own sketches. Eaton's would draft the customer's design, send the customer a quote, and then, once the order was placed, provide blueprints.

Six-room homes were common, but there were also two-storey homes. In the huge, two-storey Earlscourt design, even the third-floor attic contained three good-sized bedrooms. Some homes sported verandas and parlours, and a few featured bay windows.

The elegant Norland design, owned

by the Daniels and erected on their farm just outside of Lethbridge, was ordered from Minneapolis. Thanks to a cistern in the basement, water could be pumped upstairs. There was electricity and an electric chandelier. The house's built-in vacuum was ahead of its time, but it was cumbersome, and eventually the Daniels bought a mobile electric vacuum.[20]

Settlers could also buy barns from catalogues, as well as hog barns, ice houses, milk houses, poultry sheds, and garages. Outhouses cost twenty-five dollars each prior to the First World War.

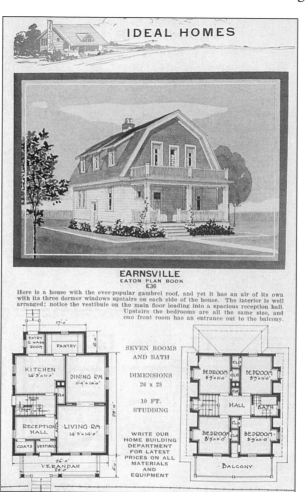

Eaton's Ideal Home, c. 1918. This house plan was large and practical but less extravagant than the Eardsley or Eager plan. In 1911, one-storey homes from the CPR cost about $950. Standard barns cost about $1000.

City of Edmonton Archives

Unique Approaches to Settling In

Early prairie homes and the possessions within ranged widely from unbelievably humble to surprisingly elegant, because there were just so many variables during the pioneer era. Some settlers had money, while others were extremely poor. Newcomers imported house-building and housekeeping traditions from all sorts of cultures. Landscape, climate, and natural building materials differed as the pioneers pushed west and north over the years. Some folks built from scratch; others ordered a house kit through the mail. Styles and circumstances changed throughout the settlement period, which stretched from the late 1800s until the 1930s.

Some newcomers lived temporarily in apartments and townhouses, such as this one in Winnipeg, and some made them their permanent homes. Provincial Archives of Manitoba Winnipeg-Homes-Terrace 7

Stories and actual buildings from the long-ago prairies can mentally transport us to the olden days. We can put ourselves in the moccasins of a Native family as they arrive at a seasonal village site. Maybe they are attracted by a buffalo herd, plentiful fur-bearing animals, a good fishing stream, a ripe berry patch, or herbs needed for a medicine woman's home remedy. They haul their belongings out of hide boxes and assemble the sweetly smoke-scented teepee. They have settled once more.

We can also imagine the loneliness of a Danish immigrant separated from his family in the Old Country or, for that matter, anyone who speaks his language and understands his traditions. At the end of a long day building his homestead, he might have no one to share a meal with, no one to hear his story about a hawk nabbing a baby rabbit right before his eyes, no one to listen as he complains about his sore back. We can sense his happiness and relief at being joined by Danish neighbours, and his enthusiasm in helping them build near his new home.

We can feel the exhaustion of a woman with young children in a sod house. In our minds we watch her struggle with her many job descriptions: she is housekeeper, educator, doctor, gardener, pest exterminator, and livestock manager. In what moments she can steal from other jobs, she hangs wallpaper or curtains over the black walls. On rainy days, she and her husband and children sit cooped up in the dark soddie, avoiding the dirty drips from the ceiling, slipping on the sloppy floor, watching the wallpaper sag and worms poke their heads (or their tails?) through the walls. On fair days, they work like the

Built of hewn logs and beautifully thatched, this home became a museum at Shandro, near Edmonton. Today, its future is very uncertain, and it appears the building will fall into dissolution. The public can visit a thatched-roof home at Elk Island Park, near Edmonton's Ukrainian Cultural Village.
Provincial Archives of Alberta A 1640

dickens, broiling their faces in the hot wind and turning their hands to sandpaper as they struggle to build a log or lumber home.

During the hardships, the times of sickness and death, when they were freezing or sweltering in homes without electricity, sanitation, and running water, all of these people—who had such promising dreams at the start—must have felt deep disappointment. They must have felt crushed by profound fatigue and heartache. But there must have been golden days, too, days when the sun sparkled on the snow, and each family felt cozy and secure in their home-made house. There must have been springs when the frogs croaked in the slough and the songbirds made nests, and summers and autumns when the crop was good, days when the children giggled and chased the squawking, flustered chickens, or the smell of baking bread wafted from the outdoor oven. There must have been evenings when parents and children looked at each other in the soft lamplight and were deeply thankful. There must have been hundreds of times when these prairie people gazed across the vista of rippling grass or tilled fields and pinched themselves to make sure this heaven was real. The land was theirs. This was their home.

Present-day visitors are welcome to explore this rich history by touring early dwellings preserved in many prairie communities. Numerous parks, museums, heritage homes, and other sites are devoted to telling the settlement saga to future generations:

ALBERTA

Fort Edmonton Park shows aspects of the fur trade and relevant housing in the West from as early as 1846.

The Ukrainian Cultural Village near Edmonton includes restored homes, churches, and town buildings erected by Ukrainians from 1890 to 1930.

Heritage Park, Calgary, displays a variety of early housing, as well as a small sod structure.

Fort Calgary and nearby Deane House reveal both the basic and elegant housing of early Mounties.

SASKATCHEWAN

The Diefenbaker Homestead, Regina, is the boyhood home of former prime minister John Diefenbaker. Displays include family artifacts dating to the early 1900s.

Regina's Government House reveals the elegance of the official residence of the Lieutenant-Governor from 1891 to 1945.

The Marr Residence in Saskatoon dates back to 1884 and is one of the first homes in the community.

The Western Development Museum, Saskatoon, invites visitors to view a range of historical buildings and homes.

MANITOBA

In Churchill, the Prince of Wales Fort National Historic Site is a stone fortress built by the Hudson's Bay Company between 1731 and 1771. It is accessible only by boat.

Riel House, Winnipeg, which is furnished in period style, was the log home of Louis Riel's mother.

Seven Oaks House in Winnipeg, assumed to be the oldest habitable house in Manitoba, has a rock foundation, hand-hewn oak timbers, and split shingles. Built between 1851 and 1853, its plaster included buffalo hair as a binding agent.

Notes

1 J.G. MacGregor, *Blankets and Beads* (Edmonton, AB:
   The Institute of Applied Art, Ltd., 1949),
   151–153.

2 Robert Hill, *Manitoba: History of Its Early Settlement,
   Development and Resources* (Toronto, ON: William
   Briggs [c. 1890]). See 38–59.

3 Nellie McClung, *Clearing in the West* (Toronto, ON:
   Thomas Allen and Son Ltd., 1935). Reprint by
   Athabasca University, 1992. For the full story, see
   38–80.

4 Michael Ewanchuk, *Reflections and Reminiscences:
   Ukrainians in Canada 1892–1992* (Winnipeg, MB:
   Michael Ewanchuk, 1995), 17–19.

5 McClung, 48–49.

6 Marchioness of Dufferin & Ava, *My Canadian Journal*
   (London: John Murray, 1891). Facsimile edition
   reprinted by Coles Publishing Company, Toronto,
   1971, 320–321.

7 Ibid., 333.

8 Emily Ferguson, *Janey Canuck in the West* (London, New
   York, Toronto, Melbourne: Cassell and Company
   Ltd., 1910), 50–57.

9 Ibid., 14.

10 Rev. L. Norman Tucker, *Western Canada Handbook of
   English Church Expansion* (Toronto, ON: Musson
   Book Company, Ltd. [c. 1907]), 125–126.

11 John Blue, *Alberta: Past and Present*, Vol. I (Chicago, IL:
   Pioneer Historical Publishing Company, 1924), 200.

12 Wm. Pearson Company Album, Settlement 1912–1914,
   Provincial Archives of Manitoba, 227–230.

13 Norman Black, *A History of Saskatchewan and the Old
   North West* (Regina, SK: North West Historical
   Company, 1913), 497–498.

14 *Beiseker's Golden Heritage* (Calgary, AB: Beiseker
   Historical Society, 1977). For the Calgary
   Colonization Company, see 17–19. For the
   Uffelman story, see 434–435.

15 John Hawkes, *The Story of Saskatchewan and Its People*,
   Vol. II (Chicago–Regina: The S.J. Clarke Publishing
   Co., 1924). For the Sumner Colony, see 793–799.
   For the Barr Colony, see 761–768.

16 John MacGregor, *North-West of Sixteen* (Toronto, ON:
   McClelland & Stewart, Ltd., 1958). See 20–44.

17 J.A. Rankel, "Homesteading: sod house and wild oxen,"
   The Tribune, Provincial Archives of Manitoba,
   Clipping File, Homestead—Pioneers.

18 Liz Deering, Taped interview with the author, Red Deer,
   AB, 15 April 1999.

19 Barry Broadfoot, *Next-Year Country* (Toronto, ON: A Douglas
   Gibson Book, McClelland and Stewart, 1988), 29–32.

20 *McLean School District #2900 1913–1946* (No city:
   McLean History Book Society [c. 1987]).

DEDICATION

With love to my mother-in-law, Ada Holt, who arrived in Alberta as an infant in 1907.

ACKNOWLEDGEMENTS

*Special thanks to Ruby Reineberg, Liz Deering, Sharon Uffelman, the Canadian National Railroad,
Adrian Paton, and the McClung family.*

Select Bibliography

Beiseker's Golden Heritage. Calgary, AB: Beiseker Historical Society, 1977.

Black, Norman. *A History of Saskatchewan and the Old North West*. Regina, SK: North West Historical Company, 1913.

Blue, John. *Alberta: Past and Present*, Vol. I. Chicago, IL: Pioneer Historical Publishing Company, 1924.

Broadfoot, Barry. *Next-Year Country*. Toronto, ON: A Douglas Gibson Book, McClelland and Stewart, 1988.

Dempsey, Hugh. *Calgary—Spirit of the West*. Saskatoon, SK: Glenbow and Fifth House Publishers, 1994.

Dufferin & Ava, Marchioness of. *My Canadian Journal*. London: John Murray, 1891. Facsimile edition reprinted by Coles Publishing Company, Toronto, 1971.

Ewanchuk, Michael. *Reflections and Reminiscences: Ukrainians in Canada 1892–1992*. Winnipeg, MB: Michael Ewanchuk, 1995.

Ferguson, Emily. *Janey Canuck in the West*. London, New York, Toronto, Melbourne: Cassell and Company Ltd., 1910.

Hawkes, John. *The Story of Saskatchewan and Its People*, Vol. II. Chicago-Regina: The S.J. Clarke Publishing Co., 1924.

Hill, Robert. *Manitoba: History of Its Early Settlement, Development and Resources*. Toronto, ON: William Briggs [c. 1890].

Laubin, Reginold and Gladys. *The Indian Tipi: its history, construction and use*. Norman, OK: University of Oklahoma, Press, 1977.

Macoun, John. *Manitoba and the Great North-West*. Guelph, ON: The World Publishing Company, 1882.

MacDonald, Janice. *The Northwest Fort: Fort Edmonton*. Edmonton, AB: Lone Pine Publishing, 1983.

MacGregor, J.G. *Blankets and Beads*. Edmonton, AB: The Institute of Applied Art, Ltd., 1949.

MacGregor, John G. *North-West of Sixteen*. Toronto, ON: McClelland & Stewart Ltd., 1958.

McClung, Nellie. *Clearing in the West*. Toronto, ON: Thomas Allen and Son Ltd., 1935. Reprint by Athabasca University, 1992.

McLean School District #2900 1913–1946. No city: McLean History Book Society [c. 1987].

MacRae, Archibald Oswald. *History of the Province of Alberta*. No city: Western Canada History Co., 1912.

Nabokov, Peter, and Robert Easton. *Native American Architecture*. New York and Oxford: Oxford University Press, 1989.

Norton, Wayne. *Help Us to a Better Land: Crofter Colonies in the Prairie West*. Regina, SK: Canadian Plains Research Centre, 1994.

Prairie Trails to Blacktop: Carlyle and District 1882–1982. Carlyle, SK: Carlyle and District Historical Society, 1982.

Red Deer Advocate, 19 June 1963.

Taggart, Kathleen. "The First Shelter of Early Pioneers," *Saskatchewan History*, vol. IX, no. 3 (Autumn, 1958): 81–93.

Tucker, Rev. L. Norman. *Western Canada Handbook of English Church Expansion*. Toronto, ON: Musson Book Company, Ltd. [c. 1907].

Wetherell, Donald, and Irene Kmet. *Homes in Alberta. Building Trends, and Design 1870–1967*. Edmonton, AB: University of Alberta Press, Alberta Culture and Multiculturalism, and Alberta Municipal Affairs, 1991.

Williams, Vicky. *Calgary Then and Now*. Vancouver, BC: Bodima Books, 1978.

Winnipeg Free Press, 28 October 1961, 27 June 1967, 20 February 1971.

Yue, David and Charlotte. *The Tipi*. New York: Alfred A Knopf, 1984.

Archival Sources and Taped Interviews

Liz Deering, Taped interview with the author. Red Deer, AB: 15 April 1999.

Wm. Pearson Company Album, Settlement 1912–1914. Provincial Archives of Manitoba, 227–230.

J.A. Rankel, "Homesteading: sod house and wild oxen," *The Tribune*. Provincial Archives of Manitoba, Clipping File: Homestead—Pioneers.

Eaton House Plan Book. Winnipeg, MB: T. Eaton Co. [c. 1918]. City of Edmonton Archives.

Front cover painting (detail) reproduced from an original oil painting entitled *Prairie Homestead*, by Hubert J. Theroux, Winnipeg, Manitoba

Back cover image, home in Arcola, Saskatchewan, c. 1915, courtesy South Saskatchewan Photo Museum

Image, page i, settler's homestead near Lloydminster, Saskatchewan, 1906, courtesy Saskatchewan Archives Board R–B 2760

Cover and interior design by Brian Smith / Articulate Eye

We acknowledge the support of The Canada Council for the Arts for our publishing program.

THE CANADA COUNCIL | LE CONSEIL DES ARTS
FOR THE ARTS | DU CANADA
SINCE 1957 | DEPUIS 1957

We acknowledge the financial support of the Government of Canada through the Book Publishing Industry Development Program for our publishing activities.

Printed in Canada

99 00 01 02 03 / 5 4 3 2 1

CANADIAN CATALOGUING IN PUBLICATION DATA

Reineberg Holt, Faye.
Settling in

(Prairie Heritage series)
Includes bibliographical references.
ISBN 1-894004-34-5

1. Dwellings–Prairie Provinces–History.
2. Architecture, Domestic–Prairie Provinces–History 3. Dwellings–Prairie Provinces–History–Pictorial works
4. Architecture, Domestic–Prairie Provinces–History–Pictorial works I. Title. II. Series
NA7242.P6R44 1999   728'.09712   C99-910663-5

FIFTH
HOUSE
PUBLISHERS

FIFTH HOUSE LTD.
#9 6125 - 11th Street SE
Calgary, AB, Canada T2H 2L6